2nd Series

Sudoku

The Number Puzzle Sweeping The Nation! #4

Published by Playmore Inc., Publishers, 58 Main Street,
2nd Floor, Hackensack, N.J. 07601
and Waldman Publishing Corp., New York, New York

Printed in Canada

GETTING STARTED

Each sudoku puzzle is a 9 by 9 grid of horizontal and vertical rows, evenly separated into 9 squares with 9 spaces each. Instead of word clues, each puzzle's solution is determined by the pattern of the numbers already filled in. You solve the puzzle by filling in the missing digits so that, when completed, each row and each square will have all the numbers from 1 to 9; each number will appear in exactly nine spaces within each puzzle.

All three elements of the sudoku puzzle must be considered simultaneously: the horizontal rows, the vertical rows, and the 9 squares. You need to fill in each square with the numbers 1 through 9, but their location depends on where along each vertical and horizontal row these numbers already appear. Remember each number can be filled in only once on each horizontal and each vertical line.

Start by examining the "clues"–those numbers already filled in. They determine where each of the other numbers may and, more importantly, may not be filled in. Often by using a process of elimination, you can rule out where certain numbers can't go and thereby narrow the choices for where they can go. It isn't necessary to start with the number 1 or even with the first square, but rather with the number that appears most frequently in any given sudoku, since you will find it easier to narrow down the remaining spaces in which it will appear in.

As you work through each puzzle, the final numbers will come more easily, and give you the experience needed for the progressively harder puzzles you'll encounter as you work your way through the book.

Enjoy!

SUDOKU #1

7				3				
8	5	3				2	7	6
4			6			3		
		4			5			7
	3	9	8	7	1	4	5	
5			9			1		
		8			3			4
2	4	5				9	8	3
			9					1

easy

SUDOKU #2

	2		7	1	3			
		1	4				9	
4	5					3	8	
2					8		5	3
5		3	9	7	2	4		8
1	9		5					2
	4	2					3	6
	8				1	5		
			3	4	6		2	

easy

SUDOKU #3

	7	9						3
	4	6	1	7		9		
1		2			4		7	6
9				2				
	6						3	
			5	4				8
6	1		8			3		7
		7		1	5	6	8	
2						5	9	

easy

SUDOKU #4

2	8		9			4		7
	9	5	3		6			
1		6	4				9	5
8		1						2
	3						4	
7						5		9
6	1				4	9		3
			7		9	1	5	
9		7			8		2	4

easy

SUDOKU #5

	6	2	7		3	1	9	
5			6		4	7	2	
	7		5	9			6	
			3		9	5		
				2				
		8	1		5			
	4			3	7		5	
	1	5	8		6			7
	8	7	9		1	6	4	

easy

SUDOKU #6

		7		4	2	3	8	6
		8		7		2		5
			3	8		9	1	
				1		6	2	8
		6		9		4		
4	2	3		5				
	3	5		2	9			
9		1		6		5		
6	8	2	5	3		1		

easy

SUDOKU #7

8		2				6		
	9		1					3
4	3	7			2			1
2	8		4		5			
9		3				4		2
			3		6		1	9
1			5			3	6	7
6					7		2	
		4				5		8

easy

SUDOKU #8

6		7		5	1			
	3			7		2		
	2	1	3	4				
2			5		6		9	4
		9	7		3	5		
3	5		4		2			7
				6	7	4	3	
		4		3			2	
			9	2		7		1

easy

SUDOKU #9

					7			8
	7	9						3
	3	6	4		5		2	7
	9		3		8	7	1	4
3								2
6	1	7	2		4		3	
1	4		8		6	5	7	
7						3	8	
9			1					

easy

SUDOKU #10

6		8						9
	7	3	4		1			
	4				9	1		3
8			1	2	3		9	
5			7		8			1
	2		5	9	4			6
7		6	8				5	
			3		5	6	1	
1						8		7

easy

SUDOKU #11

1			6		2	8		5
8				3			4	
4		7						
9	8	1	2	6	7	3		
			5		1			
		3	4	9	8	2	1	6
						9		7
	6		7					8
7		5	8		6			1

easy

SUDOKU #12

	7			3	6		9	4
	9				2	6	3	
8		3	4	9		5		
	5					7	4	1
				7				
	4	9					5	
		2		6	7	4		3
	1	7	2				6	
9	3		1	4			7	

easy

SUDOKU #13

1			7	9		4	8	
	5						3	7
9						2	5	1
3			5		6			4
		5	1		4	8		
6			8		9			2
7	3	2						9
5	1						7	
	4	6		1	7			5

easy

SUDOKU #14

4	8	6			2			
1	9					5		8
	7		4			1		6
	6			3	7			1
5	3		2		6		8	7
9			1	5			3	
6		8			1		9	
7		3					6	2
			6			8	1	3

easy

SUDOKU #15

			8			7		
		6			4	2	9	1
5				9		8	4	
	4				3	5	1	9
1			4		6			7
2	7	3	1				8	
	1	9		7				2
4	5	7	3			9		
		2			5			

easy

SUDOKU #16

1			7				8	
	4				8			
		8		4	9	6	3	7
2			4		7	3		
3	5		9		2		1	8
		9	8		3			2
8	1	5	2	7		4		
			5				7	
	7				4			1

easy

SUDOKU #17

8		9	6					4
		6	1				7	
	2				7			8
		2	7	6			9	
3	8	1		4		7	2	6
	9			3	2	4		
9			3				8	
	1				4	3		
7					9	1		5

easy

SUDOKU #18

9		5			2			
7		6			3	4		
1	2			4	8	9		
	3				4	6	9	
		2		9		3		
	9	7	8				2	
		9	4	8			3	5
		4	3			2		7
			6			8		9

easy

SUDOKU #19

9	3	7						
8			2				1	7
	2			9		4		
	5	8			6	1	4	2
	1						9	
7	9	4	8			5	3	
		9		3			5	
4	6				5			9
						6	7	1

easy

SUDOKU #20

			2			9	6	
				5	3		7	
		6	4	9		2	5	
1			3					6
9		7	8		4	3		5
5					6			7
	1	2		3	8	6		
	8		7	4				
	9	5			2			

easy

SUDOKU #21

		9			3		8	
		8	6	4		9	5	
	4						1	
	1		4	3	7		2	8
5			9	6	8			1
4	8		1	2	5		3	
	9						7	
	5	2		1	6	8		
	7		5			1		

easy

SUDOKU #22

1	2	6	9			5		3
7	9				8			
	4		1					2
		9	7		1			8
		7		5		4		
4			3		9	6		
6					3		7	
			6				3	4
9		4			7	2		1

easy

SUDOKU #23

	5			4	9		3	7
	6		5				9	4
				3		6		
	9	8	4			3		1
			1		7			
7		1		6	2	8		
	8		2					
1	3			8		2		
2	7		3	6		5		

easy

SUDOKU #24

4		7			8	2	3	
	9			2				
1		3			5		6	8
		9		4			8	3
		8	3		1	6		
3	4			6		5		
2	8		1			3		9
			8				5	
	5	1	7			8		4

easy

SUDOKU #25

	8			9	2			3
1			6	8		4	5	2
5				1		8	6	
	5			3				
		1	9		8	5		
				4			9	
	4	3		5				8
6	1	7		2	3			5
8			4	6			3	

easy

SUDOKU #26

				2	7		9	1
1		4	8		3			6
	2					5		3
7		5	4	1		6		
	4						1	
		6		3	5	7		8
3		8					6	
4			3		9	1		7
9			7	6				

easy

		5	3		4		1	
3	6	8	2	9			7	4
	7			8		2		
9		4					8	
				1				
	8					3		5
		6		3			2	
5	3			4	7	9	6	8
	4		6		8	1		

easy

5		7		4	2		6	
		1			5	9		
	4	3		9	7		5	
	8		3					1
	7	9				6	4	
	5				6		8	
	3		5	2		1		9
		4	9				8	
	2		7	8		4		6

easy

SUDOKU #28

2		3	9		8			
		6	2	7	3			
8		4				2	7	
	2		4			5	9	
	4		7		5		1	
	3				9		4	
	6	2				9		5
			3	5	2	1		
			6		4	7		8

easy

SUDOKU #29

2	1	9						
4			9	1				
7		3	6			4	9	
		2	1			8		
1			4	7	3			
8	3		5			2	7	
3		7	2			6	1	
				5	9			

easy

SUDOKU #31

8		1						
	9		6			5		
	6	5	9		1	4	2	8
6	5		8	7	3			
		4				8		
			4	9	5		6	2
3	4	6	1		2	9	8	
		9			4		1	
						6		4

easy

SUDOKU #32

		1			8		9	2
	3							6
			4	7	1		8	
3	6		1	5		2		
8	9		7		6		5	1
		4		2	3		7	9
	8		6	1	4			
2							6	
6	4		2			1		

easy

SUDOKU #33

	4				7		2	
	1	6	3		4			8
2			8		1		4	
		9	5		8		3	1
3				7				4
8	2		1		3	6		
	9		4		5			2
4			7		6	5	8	
	8		2				6	

easy

SUDOKU #34

	9	2	5					
	1	8	2	4	3			5
7	3	5	1	9				
	2					1		
	6			7			9	
		7					4	
				5	1	3	6	8
8			4	2	6	7	1	
					9	4	5	

easy

SUDOKU #35

1	2			8				
6	7		9	4		1		8
4		9	3		1	7		
2		1		4				
	9						5	
						4		3
		2	4		7	8		5
8		6		2	3		4	7
				6			1	2

easy

SUDOKU #36

3			2	8	6			7
9	6				4		2	
		2	5	9		4		8
		3		2				9
	9						5	
4				7		1		
5				6	2	8		
	4		9				3	6
2			8	3	1			4

easy

SUDOKU #37

	3			4				
6		4	2			8		
1	2			3	6		5	
4		1		5			9	
7			6		1			5
	6			2		1		7
	4		3	1			6	2
		3			2	4		8
				9			7	

easy

SUDOKU #38

					5			
1			9	7		4	3	
5				4	2	1		6
		3	2	1	6	7	5	
	5						4	
	9	1	7	5	4	3		
3		8	6	9				7
	1	7		2	3			4
			4					

easy

SUDOKU #39

	9		5	2		3	6	7
6				7				
	7				9		8	
9	4	6			1			5
			2		4			
8			7			1	9	4
	6		3				4	
				8				3
2	3	4		6	5		1	

easy

SUDOKU #40

	1		9		2	6	4	
		6			5			2
			4		9	5	1	
	6	5		8				
9		4	7		3	5		8
			4			2	6	
6	4	1		2				
7			3			8		
	8	3	5		4		9	

easy

SUDOKU #41

	6				3		9	
						8		
1		4			2		3	
4	2	9	7	3				5
6	1	7		5		3	4	8
8				6	4	9	2	7
	9		3			5		4
		1						
	5		6				7	

easy

SUDOKU #42

6				9		3		
1	4	3			5			7
			1	4			5	
			4			7	6	3
		6		5		2		
7	2	4			6			
	8			2	9			
2			6			5	3	8
		5		7				1

easy

SUDOKU #43

		6	9		1			3
9	5				2			1
1			4		7			
		1		4	9		2	7
		2		7		8		
	8		2	1		3		
			5		8			2
5			7				6	8
2			1		4	7		

easy

SUDOKU #44

	5			7				1
2	9	3	8					
			5	4				6
8	7				6		3	
	6	9	1		2	4	7	
	3		7				1	5
3				8	4			
					5	7	2	4
1				2			6	

easy

SUDOKU #45

	9		7				1	3
		3	2	4				
			9	1		2		7
8		5	4	2				6
9		4				5		2
2		7		3	1	8		4
3		1		6	2			
				9	5	4		
6	5				4		2	

easy

SUDOKU #46

								1
	2		7	6	5		4	
		9	2		4		8	
	7	3		4	8	6		
2		4	9		1	7		8
		1	6	2		9	3	
	8		3		9	1		
	9		1	8	6		7	
5								

easy

SUDOKU #47

		2			8	5	3	9
		3	6					
8		9	2		4		7	
	9	4		8	7	2	5	
		6				8		
	8	5	9	1		6	4	
	4		8		6	9		5
			4	1				
6	2	1	5			7		

easy

SUDOKU #48

		3	4					8
	4	5	8			7	2	
	8		1	7	5		4	
			6	1			3	9
9		1				4		6
8	3			9	4			
	9		5	4	1		6	
	1	2			6	3	7	
4					3	9		

easy

SUDOKU #49

				1		7		4
				3		5		8
7	3		5	4				6
9	4		2			6	5	
6			4		3			2
	8	1			5		9	3
3				6	8		7	1
8		7		5				
1		9		2				

easy

SUDOKU #50

	6	7	9	1			5	
			6					1
5	3	1				9	6	2
					1	3		
1	4		3	5	9		7	8
		8						
7	9	5				8	3	4
4					3			
	8			7	4	1	9	

easy

SUDOKU #51

			4	3		5	7	1
	8		1		2			
	3						6	8
	9	2				4	5	
	5		9	7	4		2	
	7	4				8	3	
2	6						1	
			2		1		8	
5	1	8		4	7			

easy

SUDOKU #52

2		7			3			5
	9		4			2		
	8		1	7		9		
3	2	9			6	1		
	6			2			5	
		5	3			6	4	2
		6		3	5		2	
		2			1		9	
1			2			7		6

easy

SUDOKU #53

7				8		1		
		6	5			3		
5	4			3	2		8	
		3		1	5			9
2			3		4			5
8			6	2		7		
	9		4	5			7	2
		4			7	5		
		7		6				1

easy

SUDOKU #54

7	2		3		8			1
			4		2			
4	8	5	1	6		3		
3	1				6	8		
	7						9	
		8	7				4	2
		1		7	4	9	5	8
		5		3				
5			8		9		3	6

easy

SUDOKU #55

	1		9					5
		9		4		6		3
		5	3	8	1		9	
2		1		5	4			7
		8	1		7	2		
9			6	2		8		1
	2		7	6	9	5		
8		7		3		1		
5					8		7	

easy

SUDOKU #56

2					8	5		
3	4				5		8	
6		8			7		2	
	3	2		7	4	9		6
		6				2		
4		9	1	2		7	3	
	2		4			6		1
	6		7				5	3
		3	6					2

easy

SUDOKU #57

		4	9					
	3	2	4	7	1			8
1			2	5				3
	4	8		3	2	1	9	
	6	1	7	4		3	8	
4				1	7			9
3			6	2	4	5	7	
				5	4			

easy

SUDOKU #58

4	3	8		6				
8	1				2	8		4
6	7	2					3	5
			9	7		6		
	8						9	
		1		4	6			
8	2					3	1	9
3		7	1				2	
				8		7	4	6

easy

SUDOKU #59

7	8	3					9	2
		4		8			1	
9	6			4			3	
		5	7				4	
1	7				4		8	6
	9				1	2		
	4			2			6	9
	1			9		8		
6	5					1	2	3

easy

SUDOKU #60

	7			3			8	
			1		8	7		3
			7		9	2	5	1
9	4			1	2			6
			9		6			
7			4	8			1	9
8	9	6	3		7			
1		5	6		4			
	3			2			9	

easy

SUDOKU #61

2	1			4	6		8	
		5		7		2		3
		8			5		9	
		4				7		
	5	3	6	2	7	1	4	
		2				8		
	9		8			3		
3				5		9		
	2		1	3			6	8

easy

SUDOKU #62

5				1				
6					7			5
	3	7	8	9		6		2
3	1				2		5	9
	5			4			7	
4	7		9				1	6
7		1		2	9	5	8	
8			5					4
				6				1

easy

SUDOKU #63

		3		1	8	4	6	
6	9	1						
		5	3		2			
		6		9	1	5	3	
1	5						4	8
	8	9	2	4		6		
			1		9	3		
					7	8	5	1
	1	8	4	5		7		

easy

SUDOKU #64

6	5		9					1
			8	7		2	4	
			1	4		5		
	8	5			9		7	4
2	9		4			8	1	
		8		9	3			
	2	7		1	4			
4					8		3	2

easy

SUDOKU #65

	9	4		8		2		
		1	9			3		6
	2		6					
		7	8	1	2	6		
		6				8		
		9	5	7	6	1		
					8		7	
1		3			9	4		
		8		6		9	2	

easy

SUDOKU #66

4	9	5						3
8		6	4				7	
	3							
6	5		8		7		1	
				9				
	7		3		2		4	9
							3	
	2				6	8		4
3						7	5	6

intermediate

SUDOKU #67

	4	2	5			6		8
		9	2					
	3	5					2	
	5			7		4		2
2		6		8			1	
	8						9	
					2	8		
1		3			4	5	6	

intermediate

SUDOKU #68

	2	5						
	6			3	8			2
			2		9		6	5
		4	3		2	1		
	7			5			8	
		8	7		4	2		
3	4		1		6			
6			8	9			3	
							2	

intermediate

SUDOKU #69

		2						
	6			8				
		4	5			7		3
				1			9	5
5	9		2		6		7	4
1	4			7				
7		5			4	3		
				5			1	
						9		

intermediate

SUDOKU #70

4	7	3						5
			5					4
		6	8					
6		9					1	
		8	6		9	2		
	3					4		6
			7		3	8		
3					5			
5						6	2	3

intermediate

SUDOKU #71

8		6						
					7		5	6
	1	7			9	2		
9		5		7				
	4	3				5	7	
				5		4		1
		1	7			8	3	
7	9		4					
						7		5

intermediate

SUDOKU #72

			5				8	
2		3			8		7	
		8				4	1	
1					4		9	
9			3	2	6			7
	7		8					4
	2	1				9		
	6		9			7		2
					3			

intermediate

SUDOKU #73

	9							2
5		2	1	6		9		
			9			6		
	1					8	9	3
		9				2		
7	4	8					6	
		7		8				
		3		2	6	7		9
6							4	

intermediate

SUDOKU #74

2		6				9		
				7		2		
			9	5				1
1				9		8		5
	8						7	
3		7		6				4
6				3	7			
		8		1				
		4				7		6

intermediate

SUDOKU #75

2				8				3
	8		2		1			
		1	6		5		2	
					7			
3		8		6		7		9
			9					
	9		7		8	2		
			5		4		1	
4				9				8

intermediate

SUDOKU #76

		1					8	
		6	5		8			7
				3	6			5
6			4			8		
8	4			7			5	6
		3			5			2
7			9	1				
3			7		4	9		
	2					7		

intermediate

SUDOKU #77

								5
			4		9		2	
1	4		7				6	9
3		8		1				
		4	3		6	7		
				8		4		2
4	6				8		9	3
	5		1		2			
2								

intermediate

SUDOKU #78

		5			9			7
		3			5		8	4
6					8		5	
		7			3	8		
	3						1	2
		4	6			5		
	7		9					8
3	6		7			1		
4			8			2		

intermediate

SUDOKU #79

	1		3					4
		4				5		
2		5			4	3	6	9
				7			5	
4			2		3			8
	8			6				
1	4	8	7			6		5
		7				1		
5					2		4	

intermediate

SUDOKU #80

		9		7				
7		4		6	1			
1	6				5	7		
8		3					9	
	2						8	
	7					2		3
		8	2				1	9
			8	1		4		6
				9		3		

intermediate

SUDOKU #81

7			3		5		1	2
						8	3	7
	2			8		5	9	
				9		3		
			4		8			
		9		1			7	
	6	4		7			8	
9	8	5						
1	7		8		3			6

intermediate

SUDOKU #82

3					5			4
			3	8		2		
2	8			4			9	1
5			8					2
	2		7		6		4	
6					1			9
9	3			7			1	6
		4		1	3			
8			9					7

intermediate

SUDOKU #83

			4	5				
2	5					8		
9		4			7			3
		1	2			6	9	
			6		9			
	9	5			3	1		
1			5			9		4
		8					2	1
				3	4			

intermediate

SUDOKU #84

	1			4				
						2	8	
6		5			1			4
		8	2		7		9	
							3	
	5		8		6	1		
1			4			6		9
	8	9						
				5			2	

intermediate

SUDOKU #85

							3	9
9	4	3		7		6		
7				6				8
	1	6			7	3		
3	9						1	7
		4	9			8	6	
6				9				3
		7		2		9	8	6
2	5							

intermediate

SUDOKU #86

5		9	6					3
				5			6	
		3		2	4			
	9			3		5	7	4
4	8	5		7			2	
			5	4		1		
	4			9				
6					2	4		8

intermediate

SUDOKU #87

	3	5	6	7				
	2	7			5			
9	6							
				3			9	2
5		1				8		4
3	8			9				
							5	8
			8			4	1	
				4	9	3	6	

intermediate

SUDOKU #88

								6
	8	4	7		6	5		
			5	3				7
3		7						8
			6	5	9			
2						4		5
5				6	1			
		2	4		5	6	8	
4								

intermediate

SUDOKU #89

						5	1	
3			5			8		
		8	1	2	3			6
	8							
6	7	1				4	3	2
							7	
1			8	4	7	3		
		6			5			7
	5	7						

intermediate

SUDOKU #90

		6		3				7
	2		9				6	
3	5							4
5						2		
		3	5		7	8		
		9						6
8							1	3
	4				9		5	
1				7		6		

intermediate

SUDOKU #91

3			5					
	9					7	4	5
7				6			3	
	1				4	2		8
			6		8			
4		2	9				5	
	5			9				7
2	7	9					6	
					5			3

challenging

SUDOKU #92

	3	4		5				
5				1		4		
	9				2		7	
					5	2	4	
	7						3	
	4	9	1					
	5		7				9	
		8		6				7
				2		6	5	

challenging

SUDOKU #93

8			3	2	7	9		
		2			1	4		
			5					2
	5	8	7	6			2	
				3				
	6			5	2	7	8	
2					6			
		5	2				6	
		6	4	9	5			7

challenging

SUDOKU #94

			5			7		2
				2	4		8	
			6		1			
8	6			3		2		
2	3						5	6
		9		8			7	4
			8		7			
	9		4	6				
1		3			2			

challenging

SUDOKU #95

	9	8			5			
5		2			3			7
		3				5		1
				7			5	4
			5		6			
7	8			9	2			
8		9				4		
3			6			8		5
			8			1	3	

challenging

SUDOKU #96

		8						
				6	2			8
6			4			5	3	
	3				1	4		2
	9						7	
5		4	2				1	
	8	2			3			1
3			7	8				
						7		

tough

SUDOKU #97

	8		4	7				
	7	4						
		5	6		1			
6				4			7	1
	4	7		9		2	3	
5	1			2				9
			2		9	7		
						5	9	
				5	7		6	

tough

SUDOKU #98

	6	4	8					
		9		4	6			5
7				5			8	6
						7	3	
8	1			3			6	4
	9	3						
1	5			8				7
9			6	7		5		
					5	8	4	

tough

SUDOKU #99

		5		7		4		6
	1		3					8
				9			2	
		1	6					9
			9	5	4			
					7	6		
	8		4					
3					5		4	
1		6		9		7		

super tough

SUDOKU #100

						4		
7		4		9			6	
	8				6		5	1
				3	8			2
4			5		1			8
3			6	7				
8	3		1				7	
	4			8		1		6
		7						

super tough

ANSWER KEYS

SUDOKU #1

7	6	1	5	3	2	8	4	9
8	5	3	1	4	9	2	7	6
4	9	2	6	8	7	3	1	5
1	8	4	3	2	5	6	9	7
6	3	9	8	7	1	4	5	2
5	2	7	9	6	4	1	3	8
9	1	8	2	5	3	7	6	4
2	4	5	7	1	6	9	8	3
3	7	6	4	9	8	5	2	1

SUDOKU #2

8	2	9	7	1	3	6	4	5
6	3	1	4	8	5	2	9	7
4	5	7	6	2	9	3	8	1
2	7	4	1	6	8	9	5	3
5	6	3	9	7	2	4	1	8
1	9	8	5	3	4	7	6	2
9	4	2	8	5	7	1	3	6
3	8	6	2	9	1	5	7	4
7	1	5	3	4	6	8	2	9

SUDOKU #3

8	7	9	2	5	6	4	1	3
3	4	6	1	7	8	9	2	5
1	5	2	9	3	4	8	7	6
9	8	1	6	2	3	7	5	4
5	6	4	7	8	1	2	3	9
7	2	3	5	4	9	1	6	8
6	1	5	8	9	2	3	4	7
4	9	7	3	1	5	6	8	2
2	3	8	4	6	7	5	9	1

SUDOKU #4

2	8	3	9	5	1	4	6	7
4	9	5	3	7	6	2	8	1
1	7	6	4	8	2	3	9	5
8	4	1	6	9	5	7	3	2
5	3	9	2	1	7	8	4	6
7	6	2	8	4	3	5	1	9
6	1	8	5	2	4	9	7	3
3	2	4	7	6	9	1	5	8
9	5	7	1	3	8	6	2	4

SUDOKU #5

4	6	2	7	8	3	1	9	5
5	9	3	6	1	4	7	2	8
8	7	1	5	9	2	4	6	3
1	2	4	3	7	9	5	8	6
7	5	6	4	2	8	3	1	9
9	3	8	1	6	5	2	7	4
6	4	9	2	3	7	8	5	1
2	1	5	8	4	6	9	3	7
3	8	7	9	5	1	6	4	2

SUDOKU #6

1	5	7	9	4	2	3	8	6
3	9	8	6	7	1	2	4	5
2	6	4	3	8	5	9	1	7
5	7	9	4	1	3	6	2	8
8	1	6	2	9	7	4	5	3
4	2	3	8	5	6	7	9	1
7	3	5	1	2	9	8	6	4
9	4	1	7	6	8	5	3	2
6	8	2	5	3	4	1	7	9

SUDOKU #7

8	1	2	9	7	3	6	4	5
5	9	6	1	8	4	2	7	3
4	3	7	6	5	2	9	8	1
2	8	1	4	9	5	7	3	6
9	6	3	7	1	8	4	5	2
7	4	5	3	2	6	8	1	9
1	2	8	5	4	9	3	6	7
6	5	9	8	3	7	1	2	4
3	7	4	2	6	1	5	9	8

SUDOKU #8

6	8	7	2	5	1	9	4	3
4	3	5	6	7	9	2	1	8
9	2	1	3	4	8	6	7	5
2	7	8	5	1	6	3	9	4
1	4	9	7	8	3	5	6	2
3	5	6	4	9	2	1	8	7
5	1	2	8	6	7	4	3	9
7	9	4	1	3	5	8	2	6
8	6	3	9	2	4	7	5	1

SUDOKU #9

5	2	1	9	3	7	4	6	8
4	7	9	6	8	2	1	5	3
8	3	6	4	1	5	9	2	7
2	9	5	3	6	8	7	1	4
3	8	4	7	5	1	6	9	2
6	1	7	2	9	4	8	3	5
1	4	3	8	2	6	5	7	9
7	6	2	5	4	9	3	8	1
9	5	8	1	7	3	2	4	6

SUDOKU #10

6	1	8	2	3	7	5	4	9
9	7	3	4	5	1	2	6	8
2	4	5	6	8	9	1	7	3
8	6	7	1	2	3	4	9	5
5	9	4	7	6	8	3	2	1
3	2	1	5	9	4	7	8	6
7	3	6	8	1	2	9	5	4
4	8	9	3	7	5	6	1	2
1	5	2	9	4	6	8	3	7

SUDOKU #11

1	3	9	6	4	2	8	7	5
8	5	6	9	7	3	1	4	2
4	2	7	1	8	5	6	9	3
9	8	1	2	6	7	3	5	4
6	4	2	5	3	1	7	8	9
5	7	3	4	9	8	2	1	6
2	1	8	3	5	4	9	6	7
3	6	4	7	1	9	5	2	8
7	9	5	8	2	6	4	3	1

SUDOKU #12

2	7	5	8	3	6	1	9	4
1	9	4	7	5	2	6	3	8
8	6	3	4	9	1	5	2	7
3	5	8	6	2	9	7	4	1
6	2	1	5	7	4	3	8	9
7	4	9	3	1	8	2	5	6
5	8	2	9	6	7	4	1	3
4	1	7	2	8	3	9	6	5
9	3	6	1	4	5	8	7	2

SUDOKU #13

1	2	3	7	9	5	4	8	6
4	5	8	2	6	1	9	3	7
9	6	7	4	8	3	2	5	1
3	8	1	5	2	6	7	9	4
2	9	5	1	7	4	8	6	3
6	7	4	8	3	9	5	1	2
7	3	2	6	5	8	1	4	9
5	1	9	3	4	2	6	7	8
8	4	6	9	1	7	3	2	5

SUDOKU #14

4	8	6	5	1	2	3	7	9
1	9	2	7	6	3	5	4	8
3	7	5	4	8	9	1	2	6
8	6	4	9	3	7	2	5	1
5	3	1	2	4	6	9	8	7
9	2	7	1	5	8	6	3	4
6	4	8	3	2	1	7	9	5
7	1	3	8	9	5	4	6	2
2	5	9	6	7	4	8	1	3

SUDOKU #15

9	2	4	8	6	1	7	3	5
7	8	6	5	3	4	2	9	1
5	3	1	2	9	7	8	4	6
6	4	8	7	2	3	5	1	9
1	9	5	4	8	6	3	2	7
2	7	3	1	5	9	6	8	4
3	1	9	6	7	8	4	5	2
4	5	7	3	1	2	9	6	8
8	6	2	9	4	5	1	7	3

SUDOKU #16

1	3	6	7	2	5	9	8	4
9	4	7	6	3	8	1	2	5
5	2	8	1	4	9	6	3	7
2	8	1	4	5	7	3	6	9
3	5	4	9	6	2	7	1	8
7	6	9	8	1	3	5	4	2
8	1	5	2	7	6	4	9	3
4	9	3	5	8	1	2	7	6
6	7	2	3	9	4	8	5	1

SUDOKU #17

8	7	9	6	2	3	5	1	4
4	3	6	1	5	8	9	7	2
1	2	5	4	9	7	6	3	8
5	4	2	7	6	1	8	9	3
3	8	1	9	4	5	7	2	6
6	9	7	8	3	2	4	5	1
9	5	4	3	1	6	2	8	7
2	1	8	5	7	4	3	6	9
7	6	3	2	8	9	1	4	5

SUDOKU #18

9	4	5	1	6	2	7	8	3
7	8	6	9	5	3	4	1	2
1	2	3	7	4	8	9	5	6
5	3	8	2	7	4	6	9	1
4	1	2	5	9	6	3	7	8
6	9	7	8	3	1	5	2	4
2	6	9	4	8	7	1	3	5
8	5	4	3	1	9	2	6	7
3	7	1	6	2	5	8	4	9

SUDOKU #19

9	3	7	1	4	8	2	6	5
8	4	5	2	6	3	9	1	7
1	2	6	5	9	7	4	8	3
3	5	8	9	7	6	1	4	2
6	1	2	3	5	4	7	9	8
7	9	4	8	1	2	5	3	6
2	7	9	6	3	1	8	5	4
4	6	1	7	8	5	3	2	9
5	8	3	4	2	9	6	7	1

SUDOKU #20

3	5	1	2	8	7	9	6	4
2	4	9	6	5	3	8	7	1
8	7	6	4	9	1	2	5	3
1	2	8	3	7	5	4	9	6
9	6	7	8	1	4	3	2	5
5	3	4	9	2	6	1	8	7
7	1	2	5	3	8	6	4	9
6	8	3	7	4	9	5	1	2
4	9	5	1	6	2	7	3	8

SUDOKU #21

1	6	9	2	5	3	4	8	7
7	3	8	6	4	1	9	5	2
2	4	5	8	7	9	3	1	6
9	1	6	4	3	7	5	2	8
5	2	3	9	6	8	7	4	1
4	8	7	1	2	5	6	3	9
6	9	1	3	8	4	2	7	5
3	5	2	7	1	6	8	9	4
8	7	4	5	9	2	1	6	3

SUDOKU #22

1	2	6	9	7	4	5	8	3
7	9	5	2	3	8	1	4	6
8	4	3	1	6	5	7	9	2
2	6	9	7	4	1	3	5	8
3	1	7	8	5	6	4	2	9
4	5	8	3	2	9	6	1	7
6	8	2	4	1	3	9	7	5
5	7	1	6	9	2	8	3	4
9	3	4	5	8	7	2	6	1

SUDOKU #23

8	5	2	6	4	9	1	3	7
3	6	7	5	1	2	8	9	4
4	1	9	8	7	3	5	6	2
6	9	8	4	2	5	3	7	1
5	2	3	1	8	7	6	4	9
7	4	1	9	3	6	2	8	5
9	8	6	2	5	4	7	1	3
1	3	5	7	9	8	4	2	6
2	7	4	3	6	1	9	5	8

SUDOKU #24

4	6	7	9	1	8	2	3	5
8	9	5	6	2	3	4	1	7
1	2	3	4	7	5	9	6	8
6	1	9	5	4	2	7	8	3
5	7	8	3	9	1	6	4	2
3	4	2	8	6	7	5	9	1
2	8	6	1	5	4	3	7	9
7	3	4	2	8	9	1	5	6
9	5	1	7	3	6	8	2	4

SUDOKU #25

4	8	6	5	9	2	1	7	3
1	3	9	6	8	7	4	5	2
5	7	2	3	1	4	8	6	9
9	5	4	2	3	6	7	8	1
3	6	1	9	7	8	5	2	4
7	2	8	1	4	5	3	9	6
2	4	3	7	5	9	6	1	8
6	1	7	8	2	3	9	4	5
8	9	5	4	6	1	2	3	7

SUDOKU #26

5	8	3	6	2	7	4	9	1
1	9	4	8	5	3	2	7	6
6	2	7	1	9	4	5	8	3
7	3	5	4	1	8	6	2	9
8	4	9	2	7	6	3	1	5
2	1	6	9	3	5	7	4	8
3	7	8	5	4	1	9	6	2
4	6	2	3	8	9	1	5	7
9	5	1	7	6	2	8	3	4

SUDOKU #27

5	9	7	1	4	2	3	6	8
2	6	1	8	3	5	9	7	4
8	4	3	6	9	7	2	5	1
4	8	6	3	7	9	5	1	2
1	7	9	2	5	8	6	4	3
3	5	2	4	1	6	7	8	9
6	3	8	5	2	4	1	9	7
7	1	4	9	6	3	8	2	5
9	2	5	7	8	1	4	3	6

SUDOKU #28

2	7	3	9	4	8	6	5	1
5	1	6	2	7	3	4	8	9
8	9	4	5	6	1	2	7	3
1	2	8	4	3	6	5	9	7
6	4	9	7	8	5	3	1	2
7	3	5	1	2	9	8	4	6
4	6	2	8	1	7	9	3	5
9	8	7	3	5	2	1	6	4
3	5	1	6	9	4	7	2	8

SUDOKU #29

6	1	9	3	2	5	8	4	7
4	5	8	9	1	7	2	3	6
7	2	3	6	8	4	9	1	5
5	7	2	1	9	8	3	6	4
1	9	6	4	7	3	5	8	2
8	3	4	5	6	2	7	9	1
3	8	7	2	4	6	1	5	9
2	4	1	8	5	9	6	7	3
9	6	5	7	3	1	4	2	8

SUDOKU #30

2	9	5	3	7	4	8	1	6
3	6	8	2	9	1	5	7	4
4	7	1	5	8	6	2	3	9
9	2	4	7	5	3	6	8	1
6	5	3	8	1	9	7	4	2
1	8	7	4	6	2	3	9	5
8	1	6	9	3	5	4	2	7
5	3	2	1	4	7	9	6	8
7	4	9	6	2	8	1	5	3

SUDOKU #31

8	2	1	5	4	7	3	9	6
4	9	3	6	2	8	5	7	1
7	6	5	9	3	1	4	2	8
6	5	2	8	7	3	1	4	9
9	7	4	2	1	6	8	3	5
1	3	8	4	9	5	7	6	2
3	4	6	1	5	2	9	8	7
5	8	9	7	6	4	2	1	3
2	1	7	3	8	9	6	5	4

SUDOKU #32

5	7	1	3	6	8	4	9	2
4	3	8	5	9	2	7	1	6
9	2	6	4	7	1	5	8	3
3	6	7	1	5	9	2	4	8
8	9	2	7	4	6	3	5	1
1	5	4	8	2	3	6	7	9
7	8	3	6	1	4	9	2	5
2	1	5	9	3	7	8	6	4
6	4	9	2	8	5	1	3	7

SUDOKU #33

5	4	8	9	6	7	1	2	3
9	1	6	3	2	4	7	5	8
2	7	3	8	5	1	9	4	6
7	6	9	5	4	8	2	3	1
3	5	1	6	7	2	8	9	4
8	2	4	1	9	3	6	7	5
6	9	7	4	8	5	3	1	2
4	3	2	7	1	6	5	8	9
1	8	5	2	3	9	4	6	7

SUDOKU #34

4	9	2	5	6	7	8	3	1
6	1	8	2	4	3	9	7	5
7	3	5	1	9	8	6	2	4
9	2	4	6	3	5	1	8	7
5	6	1	8	7	4	2	9	3
3	8	7	9	1	2	5	4	6
2	4	9	7	5	1	3	6	8
8	5	3	4	2	6	7	1	9
1	7	6	3	8	9	4	5	2

SUDOKU #35

1	2	3	7	8	6	5	9	4
6	7	5	9	4	2	1	3	8
4	8	9	3	5	1	7	2	6
2	3	1	5	7	4	6	8	9
7	9	4	6	3	8	2	5	1
5	6	8	2	1	9	4	7	3
3	1	2	4	9	7	8	6	5
8	5	6	1	2	3	9	4	7
9	4	7	8	6	5	3	1	2

SUDOKU #36

3	5	4	2	8	6	9	1	7
9	6	8	7	1	4	3	2	5
7	1	2	5	9	3	4	6	8
6	8	3	1	2	5	7	4	9
1	9	7	3	4	8	6	5	2
4	2	5	6	7	9	1	8	3
5	3	9	4	6	2	8	7	1
8	4	1	9	5	7	2	3	6
2	7	6	8	3	1	5	9	4

SUDOKU #37

8	3	7	1	4	5	6	2	9
6	5	4	2	7	9	8	3	1
1	2	9	8	3	6	7	5	4
4	8	1	7	5	3	2	9	6
7	9	2	6	8	1	3	4	5
3	6	5	9	2	4	1	8	7
5	4	8	3	1	7	9	6	2
9	7	3	5	6	2	4	1	8
2	1	6	4	9	8	5	7	3

SUDOKU #38

8	3	4	1	6	5	9	7	2
1	6	2	9	7	8	4	3	5
5	7	9	3	4	2	1	8	6
4	8	3	2	1	6	7	5	9
7	5	6	8	3	9	2	4	1
2	9	1	7	5	4	3	6	8
3	4	8	6	9	1	5	2	7
6	1	7	5	2	3	8	9	4
9	2	5	4	8	7	6	1	3

SUDOKU #39

4	9	1	5	2	8	3	6	7
6	8	5	1	7	3	4	2	9
3	7	2	6	4	9	5	8	1
9	4	6	8	3	1	2	7	5
1	5	7	2	9	4	8	3	6
8	2	3	7	5	6	1	9	4
5	6	8	3	1	7	9	4	2
7	1	9	4	8	2	6	5	3
2	3	4	9	6	5	7	1	8

SUDOKU #40

5	1	7	9	8	2	6	4	3
4	9	6	1	3	5	7	8	2
8	3	2	6	4	7	9	5	1
1	6	5	2	9	8	4	3	7
9	2	4	7	6	3	5	1	8
3	7	8	4	5	1	2	6	9
6	4	1	8	2	9	3	7	5
7	5	9	3	1	6	8	2	4
2	8	3	5	7	4	1	9	6

SUDOKU #41

5	6	2	8	7	3	4	9	1
9	7	3	4	1	6	8	5	2
1	8	4	5	9	2	7	3	6
4	2	9	7	3	8	1	6	5
6	1	7	2	5	9	3	4	8
8	3	5	1	6	4	9	2	7
2	9	6	3	8	7	5	1	4
7	4	1	9	2	5	6	8	3
3	5	8	6	4	1	2	7	9

SUDOKU #42

6	5	2	8	9	7	3	1	4
1	4	3	2	6	5	8	9	7
9	7	8	1	4	3	6	5	2
5	1	9	4	8	2	7	6	3
8	3	6	7	5	1	2	4	9
7	2	4	9	3	6	1	8	5
3	8	1	5	2	9	4	7	6
2	9	7	6	1	4	5	3	8
4	6	5	3	7	8	9	2	1

SUDOKU #43

8	4	6	9	5	1	2	7	3
9	5	7	6	3	2	4	8	1
1	2	3	4	8	7	6	5	9
6	3	1	8	4	9	5	2	7
4	9	2	3	7	5	8	1	6
7	8	5	2	1	6	3	9	4
3	7	9	5	6	8	1	4	2
5	1	4	7	2	3	9	6	8
2	6	8	1	9	4	7	3	5

SUDOKU #44

6	5	4	2	7	9	3	8	1
2	9	3	8	6	1	5	4	7
7	1	8	5	4	3	2	9	6
8	7	1	4	5	6	9	3	2
5	6	9	1	3	2	4	7	8
4	3	2	7	9	8	6	1	5
3	2	7	6	8	4	1	5	9
9	8	6	3	1	5	7	2	4
1	4	5	9	2	7	8	6	3

SUDOKU #45

4	9	2	7	5	8	6	1	3
1	7	3	2	4	6	9	8	5
5	8	6	9	1	3	2	4	7
8	3	5	4	2	9	1	7	6
9	1	4	6	8	7	5	3	2
2	6	7	5	3	1	8	9	4
3	4	1	8	6	2	7	5	9
7	2	8	3	9	5	4	6	1
6	5	9	1	7	4	3	2	8

SUDOKU #46

7	4	5	8	9	3	2	6	1
1	2	8	7	6	5	3	4	9
6	3	9	2	1	4	5	8	7
9	7	3	5	4	8	6	1	2
2	6	4	9	3	1	7	5	8
8	5	1	6	2	7	9	3	4
4	8	7	3	5	9	1	2	6
3	9	2	1	8	6	4	7	5
5	1	6	4	7	2	8	9	3

SUDOKU #47

4	6	2	1	7	8	5	3	9
5	1	7	3	6	9	4	2	8
8	3	9	2	5	4	1	7	6
1	9	4	6	8	7	2	5	3
2	7	6	4	3	5	8	9	1
3	8	5	9	1	2	6	4	7
7	4	3	8	2	6	9	1	5
9	5	8	7	4	1	3	6	2
6	2	1	5	9	3	7	8	4

SUDOKU #48

1	7	3	4	6	2	5	9	8
6	4	5	8	3	9	7	2	1
2	8	9	1	7	5	6	4	3
7	5	4	6	1	8	2	3	9
9	2	1	3	5	7	4	8	6
8	3	6	2	9	4	1	5	7
3	9	7	5	4	1	8	6	2
5	1	2	9	8	6	3	7	4
4	6	8	7	2	3	9	1	5

SUDOKU #49

5	9	2	8	1	6	7	3	4
4	1	6	7	3	9	5	2	8
7	3	8	5	4	2	9	1	6
9	4	3	2	8	1	6	5	7
6	7	5	4	9	3	1	8	2
2	8	1	6	7	5	4	9	3
3	5	4	9	6	8	2	7	1
8	2	7	1	5	4	3	6	9
1	6	9	3	2	7	8	4	5

SUDOKU #50

8	6	7	9	1	2	4	5	3
9	2	4	6	3	5	7	8	1
5	3	1	7	4	8	9	6	2
6	7	9	2	8	1	3	4	5
1	4	2	3	5	9	6	7	8
3	5	8	4	6	7	2	1	9
7	9	5	1	2	6	8	3	4
4	1	6	8	9	3	5	2	7
2	8	3	5	7	4	1	9	6

SUDOKU #51

9	2	6	4	3	8	5	7	1
7	8	5	1	6	2	9	4	3
4	3	1	7	5	9	2	6	8
6	9	2	8	1	3	4	5	7
8	5	3	9	7	4	1	2	6
1	7	4	5	2	6	8	3	9
2	6	9	3	8	5	7	1	4
3	4	7	2	9	1	6	8	5
5	1	8	6	4	7	3	9	2

SUDOKU #52

2	1	7	9	6	3	4	8	5
6	9	3	4	5	8	2	1	7
5	8	4	1	7	2	9	6	3
3	2	9	5	4	6	1	7	8
4	6	1	8	2	7	3	5	9
8	7	5	3	1	9	6	4	2
9	4	6	7	3	5	8	2	1
7	3	2	6	8	1	5	9	4
1	5	8	2	9	4	7	3	6

SUDOKU #53

7	3	2	9	8	6	1	5	4
9	8	6	5	4	1	3	2	7
5	4	1	7	3	2	9	8	6
4	7	3	8	1	5	2	6	9
2	6	9	3	7	4	8	1	5
8	1	5	6	2	9	7	4	3
1	9	8	4	5	3	6	7	2
6	2	4	1	9	7	5	3	8
3	5	7	2	6	8	4	9	1

SUDOKU #54

7	2	9	3	5	8	4	6	1
1	6	3	4	9	2	5	8	7
4	8	5	1	6	7	3	2	9
3	1	2	9	4	6	8	7	5
6	7	4	2	8	5	1	9	3
9	5	8	7	3	1	6	4	2
2	3	1	6	7	4	9	5	8
8	9	6	5	2	3	7	1	4
5	4	7	8	1	9	2	3	6

SUDOKU #55

3	1	2	9	7	6	4	8	5
7	8	9	5	4	2	6	1	3
4	6	5	3	8	1	7	9	2
2	3	1	8	5	4	9	6	7
6	5	8	1	9	7	2	3	4
9	7	4	6	2	3	8	5	1
1	2	3	7	6	9	5	4	8
8	9	7	4	3	5	1	2	6
5	4	6	2	1	8	3	7	9

SUDOKU #56

2	9	1	3	4	8	5	6	7
3	4	7	2	6	5	1	8	9
6	5	8	9	1	7	3	2	4
5	3	2	8	7	4	9	1	6
7	1	6	5	3	9	2	4	8
4	8	9	1	2	6	7	3	5
9	2	5	4	8	3	6	7	1
1	6	4	7	9	2	8	5	3
8	7	3	6	5	1	4	9	2

SUDOKU #57

8	5	4	9	6	3	2	1	7
9	3	2	4	7	1	6	5	8
1	7	6	2	5	8	9	4	3
7	4	8	5	3	2	1	9	6
5	9	3	1	8	6	7	2	4
2	6	1	7	4	9	3	8	5
4	2	5	3	1	7	8	6	9
3	8	9	6	2	4	5	7	1
6	1	7	8	9	5	4	3	2

SUDOKU #58

4	3	8	5	6	9	1	7	2
9	1	5	7	3	2	8	6	4
6	7	2	4	1	8	9	3	5
2	4	3	9	7	5	6	8	1
5	8	6	3	2	1	4	9	7
7	9	1	8	4	6	2	5	3
8	2	4	6	5	7	3	1	9
3	6	7	1	9	4	5	2	8
1	5	9	2	8	3	7	4	6

SUDOKU #59

7	8	3	5	1	6	4	9	2
5	2	4	3	8	9	6	1	7
9	6	1	2	4	7	5	3	8
8	3	5	7	6	2	9	4	1
1	7	2	9	5	4	3	8	6
4	9	6	8	3	1	2	7	5
3	4	8	1	2	5	7	6	9
2	1	7	6	9	3	8	5	4
6	5	9	4	7	8	1	2	3

SUDOKU #60

6	7	1	2	3	5	9	8	4
2	5	9	1	4	8	7	6	3
3	8	4	7	6	9	2	5	1
9	4	8	5	1	2	3	7	6
5	1	3	9	7	6	4	2	8
7	6	2	4	8	3	5	1	9
8	9	6	3	5	7	1	4	2
1	2	5	6	9	4	8	3	7
4	3	7	8	2	1	6	9	5

SUDOKU #61

2	1	9	3	4	6	5	8	7
6	4	5	9	7	8	2	1	3
7	3	8	2	1	5	6	9	4
9	6	4	5	8	1	7	3	2
8	5	3	6	2	7	1	4	9
1	7	2	4	9	3	8	5	6
4	9	1	8	6	2	3	7	5
3	8	6	7	5	4	9	2	1
5	2	7	1	3	9	4	6	8

SUDOKU #62

5	9	2	6	1	4	8	3	7
6	8	4	2	3	7	1	9	5
1	3	7	8	9	5	6	4	2
3	1	6	7	8	2	4	5	9
2	5	9	1	4	6	3	7	8
4	7	8	9	5	3	2	1	6
7	6	1	4	2	9	5	8	3
8	2	3	5	7	1	9	6	4
9	4	5	3	6	8	7	2	1

SUDOKU #63

7	2	3	9	1	8	4	6	5
6	9	1	5	7	4	2	8	3
8	4	5	3	6	2	1	7	9
4	7	6	8	9	1	5	3	2
1	5	2	7	3	6	9	4	8
3	8	9	2	4	5	6	1	7
5	6	7	1	8	9	3	2	4
9	3	4	6	2	7	8	5	1
2	1	8	4	5	3	7	9	6

SUDOKU #64

6	5	4	9	3	2	7	8	1
9	3	1	8	7	5	2	4	6
8	7	2	1	4	6	5	9	3
1	8	5	3	2	9	6	7	4
7	4	6	5	8	1	3	2	9
2	9	3	4	6	7	8	1	5
5	1	8	2	9	3	4	6	7
3	2	7	6	1	4	9	5	8
4	6	9	7	5	8	1	3	2

SUDOKU #65

6	9	4	7	8	3	2	1	5
7	8	1	9	2	5	3	4	6
3	2	5	6	4	1	7	8	9
5	3	7	8	1	2	6	9	4
2	1	6	3	9	4	8	5	7
8	4	9	5	7	6	1	3	2
9	6	2	4	3	8	5	7	1
1	7	3	2	5	9	4	6	8
4	5	8	1	6	7	9	2	3

SUDOKU #66

4	9	5	6	7	8	1	2	3
8	1	6	4	2	3	9	7	5
7	3	2	9	5	1	4	6	8
6	5	9	8	4	7	3	1	2
2	4	3	1	9	5	6	8	7
1	7	8	3	6	2	5	4	9
9	6	7	5	8	4	2	3	1
5	2	1	7	3	6	8	9	4
3	8	4	2	1	9	7	5	6

SUDOKU #67

7	4	2	5	1	9	6	3	8
6	1	9	2	3	8	7	5	4
8	3	5	6	4	7	1	2	9
3	5	1	9	7	6	4	8	2
4	9	8	1	2	5	3	7	6
2	7	6	4	8	3	9	1	5
5	8	4	7	6	1	2	9	3
9	6	7	3	5	2	8	4	1
1	2	3	8	9	4	5	6	7

SUDOKU #68

9	2	5	6	4	7	8	1	3
7	6	1	5	3	8	9	4	2
4	8	3	2	1	9	7	6	5
5	9	4	3	8	2	1	7	6
2	7	6	9	5	1	3	8	4
1	3	8	7	6	4	2	5	9
3	4	7	1	2	6	5	9	8
6	1	2	8	9	5	4	3	7
8	5	9	4	7	3	6	2	1

SUDOKU #69

3	5	2	7	4	1	8	6	9
9	6	7	3	8	2	5	4	1
8	1	4	5	6	9	7	2	3
2	7	3	4	1	8	6	9	5
5	9	8	2	3	6	1	7	4
1	4	6	9	7	5	2	3	8
7	2	5	1	9	4	3	8	6
6	3	9	8	5	7	4	1	2
4	8	1	6	2	3	9	5	7

SUDOKU #70

4	7	3	9	2	6	1	8	5
8	1	2	5	3	7	9	6	4
9	5	6	8	4	1	3	7	2
6	2	9	3	7	4	5	1	8
1	4	8	6	5	9	2	3	7
7	3	5	1	8	2	4	9	6
2	6	4	7	9	3	8	5	1
3	8	1	2	6	5	7	4	9
5	9	7	4	1	8	6	2	3

SUDOKU #71

8	3	6	5	4	2	9	1	7
4	2	9	8	1	7	3	5	6
5	1	7	3	6	9	2	4	8
9	8	5	1	7	4	6	2	3
1	4	3	6	2	8	5	7	9
6	7	2	9	5	3	4	8	1
2	5	1	7	9	6	8	3	4
7	9	8	4	3	5	1	6	2
3	6	4	2	8	1	7	9	5

SUDOKU #72

6	1	9	5	4	7	2	8	3
2	4	3	1	9	8	6	7	5
7	5	8	6	3	2	4	1	9
1	3	2	7	5	4	8	9	6
9	8	4	3	2	6	1	5	7
5	7	6	8	1	9	3	2	4
3	2	1	4	7	5	9	6	8
4	6	5	9	8	1	7	3	2
8	9	7	2	6	3	5	4	1

SUDOKU #73

1	9	6	7	8	5	4	3	2
5	3	2	1	6	4	9	8	7
8	7	4	9	3	2	6	5	1
2	1	5	6	4	7	8	9	3
3	6	9	8	5	1	2	7	4
7	4	8	2	9	3	1	6	5
9	5	7	4	1	8	3	2	6
4	8	3	5	2	6	7	1	9
6	2	1	3	7	9	5	4	8

SUDOKU #74

2	1	6	8	4	3	9	5	7
5	4	9	1	7	6	2	8	3
8	7	3	9	5	2	4	6	1
1	6	2	7	9	4	8	3	5
4	8	5	3	2	1	6	7	9
3	9	7	5	6	8	1	2	4
6	2	1	4	3	7	5	9	8
7	5	8	6	1	9	3	4	2
9	3	4	2	8	5	7	1	6

SUDOKU #75

2	7	5	4	8	9	1	6	3
6	8	3	2	7	1	4	9	5
9	4	1	6	3	5	8	2	7
1	6	9	8	4	7	3	5	2
3	5	8	1	6	2	7	4	9
7	2	4	9	5	3	6	8	1
5	9	6	7	1	8	2	3	4
8	3	7	5	2	4	9	1	6
4	1	2	3	9	6	5	7	8

SUDOKU #76

5	3	1	2	9	7	6	8	4
2	9	6	5	4	8	3	1	7
4	7	8	1	3	6	2	9	5
6	5	7	4	2	1	8	3	9
8	4	2	3	7	9	1	5	6
9	1	3	8	6	5	4	7	2
7	8	4	9	1	2	5	6	3
3	6	5	7	8	4	9	2	1
1	2	9	6	5	3	7	4	8

SUDOKU #77

6	9	7	8	2	1	3	4	5
8	3	5	4	6	9	1	2	7
1	4	2	7	3	5	8	6	9
3	7	8	2	1	4	9	5	6
9	2	4	3	5	6	7	1	8
5	1	6	9	8	7	4	3	2
4	6	1	5	7	8	2	9	3
7	5	3	1	9	2	6	8	4
2	8	9	6	4	3	5	7	1

SUDOKU #78

8	4	5	3	1	9	6	2	7
7	1	3	2	6	5	9	8	4
6	2	9	4	7	8	3	5	1
2	5	7	1	9	3	8	4	6
9	3	6	5	8	4	7	1	2
1	8	4	6	2	7	5	3	9
5	7	2	9	3	1	4	6	8
3	6	8	7	4	2	1	9	5
4	9	1	8	5	6	2	7	3

SUDOKU #79

8	1	9	3	5	6	2	7	4
3	6	4	9	2	7	5	8	1
2	7	5	1	8	4	3	6	9
9	3	2	8	7	1	4	5	6
4	5	6	2	9	3	7	1	8
7	8	1	4	6	5	9	3	2
1	4	8	7	3	9	6	2	5
6	2	7	5	4	8	1	9	3
5	9	3	6	1	2	8	4	7

SUDOKU #80

3	5	9	4	7	2	8	6	1
7	8	4	3	6	1	9	5	2
1	6	2	9	8	5	7	3	4
8	1	3	7	2	4	6	9	5
4	2	5	6	3	9	1	8	7
9	7	6	1	5	8	2	4	3
6	3	8	2	4	7	5	1	9
5	9	7	8	1	3	4	2	6
2	4	1	5	9	6	3	7	8

SUDOKU #81

7	9	8	3	4	5	6	1	2
4	5	1	6	2	9	8	3	7
6	2	3	7	8	1	5	9	4
8	4	6	2	9	7	3	5	1
5	1	7	4	3	8	2	6	9
2	3	9	5	1	6	4	7	8
3	6	4	9	7	2	1	8	5
9	8	5	1	6	4	7	2	3
1	7	2	8	5	3	9	4	6

SUDOKU #82

3	9	7	1	2	5	6	8	4
4	1	6	3	8	9	2	7	5
2	8	5	6	4	7	3	9	1
5	7	3	8	9	4	1	6	2
1	2	9	7	5	6	8	4	3
6	4	8	2	3	1	7	5	9
9	3	2	4	7	8	5	1	6
7	6	4	5	1	3	9	2	8
8	5	1	9	6	2	4	3	7

SUDOKU #83

3	8	6	4	5	2	7	1	9
2	5	7	3	9	1	8	4	6
9	1	4	8	6	7	2	5	3
4	3	1	2	8	5	6	9	7
8	7	2	6	1	9	4	3	5
6	9	5	7	4	3	1	8	2
1	6	3	5	2	8	9	7	4
5	4	8	9	7	6	3	2	1
7	2	9	1	3	4	5	6	8

SUDOKU #84

8	1	3	7	4	2	9	6	5
7	9	4	3	6	5	2	8	1
6	2	5	9	8	1	3	7	4
3	4	8	2	1	7	5	9	6
2	6	1	5	9	4	7	3	8
9	5	7	8	3	6	1	4	2
1	3	2	4	7	8	6	5	9
5	8	9	6	2	3	4	1	7
4	7	6	1	5	9	8	2	3

SUDOKU #85

1	6	8	5	4	2	7	3	9
9	4	3	8	7	1	6	2	5
7	2	5	3	6	9	1	4	8
8	1	6	2	5	7	3	9	4
3	9	2	4	8	6	5	1	7
5	7	4	9	1	3	8	6	2
6	8	1	7	9	4	2	5	3
4	3	7	1	2	5	9	8	6
2	5	9	6	3	8	4	7	1

SUDOKU #86

5	7	9	6	8	1	2	4	3
2	1	4	7	5	3	8	6	9
8	6	3	9	2	4	7	1	5
1	9	6	2	3	8	5	7	4
7	3	2	4	6	5	9	8	1
4	8	5	1	7	9	3	2	6
9	2	8	5	4	6	1	3	7
3	4	1	8	9	7	6	5	2
6	5	7	3	1	2	4	9	8

SUDOKU #87

8	3	5	6	7	4	9	2	1
1	2	7	9	8	5	6	4	3
9	6	4	2	1	3	7	8	5
7	4	6	5	3	8	1	9	2
5	9	1	7	2	6	8	3	4
3	8	2	4	9	1	5	7	6
4	1	9	3	6	7	2	5	8
6	7	3	8	5	2	4	1	9
2	5	8	1	4	9	3	6	7

SUDOKU #88

7	3	5	9	1	4	8	2	6
1	8	4	7	2	6	5	3	9
6	2	9	5	3	8	1	4	7
3	5	7	1	4	2	9	6	8
8	4	1	6	5	9	3	7	2
2	9	6	3	8	7	4	1	5
5	7	3	8	6	1	2	9	4
9	1	2	4	7	5	6	8	3
4	6	8	2	9	3	7	5	1

SUDOKU #89

7	6	2	4	8	9	5	1	3
3	1	4	5	7	6	8	2	9
5	9	8	1	2	3	7	4	6
2	8	3	7	6	4	9	5	1
6	7	1	9	5	8	4	3	2
9	4	5	3	1	2	6	7	8
1	2	9	8	4	7	3	6	5
4	3	6	2	9	5	1	8	7
8	5	7	6	3	1	2	9	4

SUDOKU #90

9	8	6	4	3	5	1	2	7
7	2	4	9	8	1	3	6	5
3	5	1	7	6	2	9	8	4
5	1	8	6	4	3	2	7	9
2	6	3	5	9	7	8	4	1
4	7	9	1	2	8	5	3	6
8	9	7	2	5	6	4	1	3
6	4	2	3	1	9	7	5	8
1	3	5	8	7	4	6	9	2

SUDOKU #91

3	2	8	5	4	7	6	1	9
6	9	1	8	3	2	7	4	5
7	4	5	1	6	9	8	3	2
9	1	6	3	5	4	2	7	8
5	3	7	6	2	8	1	9	4
4	8	2	9	7	1	3	5	6
1	5	3	2	9	6	4	8	7
2	7	9	4	8	3	5	6	1
8	6	4	7	1	5	9	2	3

SUDOKU #92

7	3	4	8	5	6	9	2	1
5	6	2	9	1	7	4	8	3
8	9	1	4	3	2	5	7	6
1	8	3	6	7	5	2	4	9
6	7	5	2	9	4	1	3	8
2	4	9	1	8	3	7	6	5
3	5	6	7	4	1	8	9	2
4	2	8	5	6	9	3	1	7
9	1	7	3	2	8	6	5	4

SUDOKU #93

8	1	4	3	2	7	9	5	6
5	9	2	6	8	1	4	7	3
6	7	3	5	4	9	8	1	2
9	5	8	7	6	4	3	2	1
4	2	7	1	3	8	5	6	9
3	6	1	9	5	2	7	8	4
2	3	9	8	7	6	1	4	5
7	4	5	2	1	3	6	9	8
1	8	6	4	9	5	2	3	7

SUDOKU #94

3	4	1	5	9	8	7	6	2
6	7	5	3	2	4	1	8	9
9	2	8	6	7	1	4	3	5
8	6	4	7	3	5	2	9	1
2	3	7	1	4	9	8	5	6
5	1	9	2	8	6	3	7	4
4	5	6	8	1	7	9	2	3
7	9	2	4	6	3	5	1	8
1	8	3	9	5	2	6	4	7

SUDOKU #95

1	9	8	7	6	5	3	4	2
5	4	2	1	8	3	9	6	7
6	7	3	9	2	4	5	8	1
9	6	1	3	7	8	2	5	4
2	3	4	5	1	6	7	9	8
7	8	5	4	9	2	6	1	3
8	5	9	2	3	1	4	7	6
3	1	7	6	4	9	8	2	5
4	2	6	8	5	7	1	3	9

SUDOKU #96

1	5	8	3	7	9	2	6	4
4	7	3	5	6	2	1	9	8
6	2	9	4	1	8	5	3	7
8	3	7	6	9	1	4	5	2
2	9	1	8	4	5	3	7	6
5	6	4	2	3	7	8	1	9
7	8	2	9	5	3	6	4	1
3	1	6	7	8	4	9	2	5
9	4	5	1	2	6	7	8	3

SUDOKU #97

1	8	6	4	7	2	9	5	3
2	7	4	9	3	5	1	8	6
9	3	5	6	8	1	4	2	7
6	2	9	5	4	3	8	7	1
8	4	7	1	9	6	2	3	5
5	1	3	7	2	8	6	4	9
3	5	8	2	6	9	7	1	4
7	6	2	3	1	4	5	9	8
4	9	1	8	5	7	3	6	2

SUDOKU #98

5	6	4	8	1	3	9	7	2
2	8	9	7	4	6	3	1	5
7	3	1	9	5	2	4	8	6
4	2	5	1	6	8	7	3	9
8	1	7	5	3	9	2	6	4
6	9	3	4	2	7	1	5	8
1	5	2	3	8	4	6	9	7
9	4	8	6	7	1	5	2	3
3	7	6	2	9	5	8	4	1

SUDOKU #99

8	3	5	2	7	1	4	9	6
2	1	9	3	4	6	5	7	8
7	6	4	5	8	9	1	2	3
4	7	1	6	3	8	2	5	9
6	2	8	9	5	4	3	1	7
9	5	3	1	2	7	6	8	4
5	8	7	4	1	3	9	6	2
3	9	2	7	6	5	8	4	1
1	4	6	8	9	2	7	3	5

SUDOKU #100

9	6	5	8	1	3	4	2	7
7	1	4	2	9	5	8	6	3
2	8	3	7	4	6	9	5	1
6	5	1	9	3	8	7	4	2
4	7	9	5	2	1	6	3	8
3	2	8	6	7	4	5	1	9
8	3	6	1	5	9	2	7	4
5	4	2	3	8	7	1	9	6
1	9	7	4	6	2	3	8	5